JASMINE TEA

P9-DHT-454

tea

discovering, exploring, enjoying

tea

discovering, exploring, enjoying

hattie ellis

photography by debi treloar

RYLAND
PETERS
& SMALL

LONDON NEW YORK

To Gordon Smith, tea-drinker

Designer Luis Peral-Aranda
Senior Editor Sophie Bevan
Picture Research Manager Kate Brunt
Production Tamsin Curwood
Art Director Gabriella Le Grazie
Publishing Director Alison Starling

Stylist Emily Chalmers
Food Stylist Fiona Smith

First published in the USA in 2002
by Ryland Peters & Small, Inc
519 Broadway, 5th Floor
New York, NY10012
www.rylandpeters.com

10 9 8 7 6 5 4 3 2

Text, design, and commissioned photographs
© Ryland Peters & Small 2002

Library of Congress Cataloging-in-Publication Data

Ellis, Hattie.
    Tea : discovering, exploring, enjoying / Hattie Ellis ;
photography by Debi Trelor.
    Includes index.
    p. cm.
    ISBN 1 84172 351 7
    1. Cookery (Tea) 2. Tea. I. Title.

TX817.T3 E43 2002
641.6372--dc21

2002021263

Printed and bound in China

contents

what is tea?

The leaves of a plant of the camellia family + hot water = tea. This simple equation sums up the most popular drink in the world. Yet this everyday drink is far from ordinary. Tea has inspired poetry and porcelain. Tea brightens mornings, refreshes afternoons, and warms nights. Tea soothes frayed nerves and stimulates tired minds. Tea brings people together around food, conversation, and hospitality. Tea has sent trading ships racing around the globe and intertwines with religion, medicine, and art.

Gathered in from lands afar, these quiet packets in our kitchen cabinets contain a world of flavors. From India, there is the subtle fineness of a single-estate Darjeeling and the chirpy vigor of an Assam; from China, a vast range of sophisticated teas, imbued with the poetry of tastes and names such as Dragon Well and Silver Needles; or the elegant jade of Japanese green teas and the scented decorum of an Earl Grey flavored with citrus bergamot oil.

In a single day, there may be three teas or blends to suit different times. In a month or a year, a dozen types can entertain your taste buds. This book, an introduction to a fascinating and delicious drink, is about how you can expand your knowledge and appreciation of tea to enjoy and explore its wide range of scents and flavors.

RIGHT Fairtrade workers harvesting tea from bushes growing on the Herkulu estate in the mountain uplands of North Tanzania, to be sold as Teadirect.

the tradition

The drinking of tea began in China, and traditions associated with it sprang up as the drink's popularity spread around the world. Different countries have evolved their own cultures of imbibing infusions of this refreshing and delicious leaf, and its influence can be seen in everything from daily domestic details through to art, literature, and history.

A brew of fragrant, first-flush leaf tea from the Castleton estate in Darjeeling, northern India, where the bushes grow in the foothills of the Himalayas.

origins

Around 4,700 years ago, so the story goes, wild tea leaves fell into a pot of boiling water. The resulting infusion was sipped by the legendary Chinese emperor Shen Nung, the Divine Healer. "It quenches thirst," he noted. "It lessens the desire for sleep. It gladdens and cheers the heart."

Another story tells how this extraordinary leaf has the power to refresh and revive. Bodhidharma, the founder of Zen Buddhism, is said to have meditated for nine years. During this period, he fell asleep and was so upset by his tiredness that he cut off his eyelids and threw them to the earth. At the spot where they fell, tea plants sprang up. From that day, the serrated ovals of tea leaves would be ever watchful against sloth.

The Chinese have woven tea into their stories, their philosophy, their art, and their literature, as well as into aspects of daily life. Successive dynasties produced different styles of tea-drinking, and sophisticated ceramics to match. Tea became a part of body, mind, spirit, and home. This Chinese passion was given a text by the eighth-century scholar, Lu Yu, whose three-volume treatise, *Classic of Tea (Ch'a Ching)*, brought together such knowledge as how to grow the plants and the use of 20 different types of water to make the brew, along with poetic descriptions of leaves that shrink and crinkle like a Mongol's boots, or swell and leap as if tossed on wind-ruffled water.

spread around the world

After being enjoyed in the East—first in China, then in Japan—for hundreds of years, tea finally reached Europe in the 17th century when Portuguese and Dutch traders brought it back as a luxury alongside silks and spices. In 1662, the Portuguese princess Catherine of Braganza included a chest of tea in her dowry when she married the British king, Charles II, and the drink became the height of sophistication among the aristocracy. Precious leaves were locked up in caddies.

And the brew was drunk from the new porcelain imported from the East, acting as ballast in the ships with the spoilable tea stored above, and named after its country of origin, "china." Meanwhile, caravans of hundreds of camels made the epic journey across mountain and desert to bring tea from China to Russia.

Tea drinking developed in America until the Boston Tea Party of 1773, when patriots threw chestfuls of tea into the sea in protest at British taxation. Tea remained relatively expensive in Europe, partly because of the distance involved in importing from China and because Europeans did not know the craft of making tea. But slowly trade developed, aided by the dark exchange of opium for tea, and in the second half of the 19th century, the famously swift clipper ships would race each other to bring the new season's teas to the West.

In the 19th century, the British Empire helped make tea a daily drink, for workers and wealthy alike, as botanists, explorers, and entrepreneurs set up tea plantations in India to develop another source of leaves and learned how to make tea. Because the water is boiled, tea is thought to have reduced urban disease and that, in turn, this safe, non-alcoholic, energizing drink helped power the advance of the Industrial Revolution.

Dr. Samuel Johnson (1704–84), who drank up to 40 cups a day, described himself as:

" ... a hardened tea-drinker, who has for twenty years diluted his meals with only the infusion of this fascinating plant; whose kettle has scarcely time to cool; who with tea amuses the evening, with tea solaces the midnight, and with tea welcomes the morning."

Camellia sinensis

tea in literature and art

Tea has long featured in the domestic scenes of art and literature. Eighteenth-century portraits depict rich families gathered around the tea table, with the porcelain and tea caddies displaying their wealth and good taste.

The calm, clean energy of tea has also refreshed and inspired writers. French authors of the 17th and 18th centuries, such as Racine, took to the new brew, as did the British. "Tea! Thou soft, thou sober, sage and venerable liquid, thou female tongue-running, smile-soothing, heart-opening, wink-tippling cordial ..." wrote Colley Cibber in 1708. The Romantic poets Coleridge and Byron wrote of tea, while Shelley downed cup after cup.

The Japanese haiku master Issa even chose to become the "cup-of-tea" poet, symbolizing how he found the beautiful in daily life. James Joyce included the plume of steam from the kettle spout and the sham Crown Derby in the domestic details of Leopold Bloom's day in *Ulysses*, and the writings of Jane Austen, Henry James, Tolstoy, Turgenev, and Thackeray all use tea as part of the events that make up life and therefore literature. In Lewis Carroll's *Alice's Adventures in Wonderland*, tea-time is given a nonsensical twist at the Mad Hatter's tea party, while Proust famously uses some crumbs of madeleine soaked in tea as a conduit to his *Remembrance of Things Past*.

the teas

Tea is one of the most natural of drinks, made simply and purely from leaves which may grow in high, clear mountain air. Yet its sophisticated range of tastes can endlessly entrance the palate as you explore its many styles from around the world.

The Chinese craft teas so that they open in the cup like flowers or stars, or roll leaves into pearls that unfurl gradually in the cup, releasing their fragrance and form.

tea plants

High on misty Himalayan mountains, tucked into the domestic plots of Chinese smallholders and in the smooth, green waves that undulate over the contours of Japanese tea gardens, grows a plant related to the garden camellia. There are two main varieties of the tea plant, *Camellia sinensis*, which provides the sweeter flavor of Chinese teas, and the Indian *Camellia assamica*.

The shiny green leaves of the tea plant are harvested regularly so the tender young tops return, again and again, vigorous and fresh with growth. The top two leaves of the plant plus the closed bud, or tip, make the finest grades. Lower leaves go into making the coarser varieties. Tea leaves can be cut and broken to make strong, tannic, quick-brewing tea, or made into subtler, more distinctive leaf teas. Especially prized, in areas with a limited growing season, are the vibrant, refreshing flavors of the first growth, or first flush, of leaves. High altitudes, with a shorter and slower growing season, make the flavor of such leaves even more intense, which is why some of the best teas grow on the mountainsides of places such as Darjeeling, where nimble women with dextrous hands balance on the steep slopes plucking the tea tips. Likewise, the high slopes of China's Yunnan province also produce fine teas. The Chinese have legendary tales of a tea grown on such inaccessible slopes that monkeys had to clamber down the mountainside to harvest the tips, illustrating their proverb, "The finest teas grow on mountainsides."

OPPOSITE, TOP ROW, FROM LEFT Castleton Darjeeling (India); Tommagong BOPF (Sri Lanka), Gyokuro (Japan).

MIDDLE ROW, FROM LEFT Fujian Phoenix Eye white tea (China); Lapsang Souchong Imperial black smoked tea (China); Hyson (China).

BOTTOM ROW, FROM LEFT Chun Mee (China); Grand Oolong (Taiwan); Gunpowder Zhy Cha green tea (China).

black, green, oolong, and white tea

All teas start from green leaves. It is the subsequent processing that determines whether they are black, green, or oolong.

Think of how autumnal leaves, deprived of their sap, wither and dry. The making of black tea is an accelerated, controlled version of this act of nature. First the plucked leaves of the tea plant are withered so they become more pliable. These partially dried leaves are then rolled to release their juices and enzymes. There follows a process of oxidation, which produces the characteristic flavor and color of black tea. Finally, the tea is fired with hot, dry air to destroy the enzymes and stabilize the leaves.

Green tea, by contrast, is made from the unoxidized leaves, which are simply heated to destroy the enzymes that would cause oxidation. They are then rolled to release their flavors and finally dried to stabilize the tea. Green tea leaves contain the sweetness and many of the vitamins and other beneficial properties of the fresh green leaf, which is why it is so highly regarded as a healthy, fragrant, and delicious drink.

Oolong teas, much loved by connoisseurs, are a cross between black and green teas, with the oxidation stopped after a short time, so they retain the freshness of green teas while taking on the subtle, sophisticated flavors and maturity of black.

Rare and precious, white teas are a Chinese specialty. The tips of the unopened leaves are carefully hand-picked while they are still furled in a silver, downy bud, and then dried. White tea is a pale, delicately fragrant infusion that is offered to honored guests. An almost spiritual drink, it is like sipping serenity.

The Indians, Sri Lankans, and Africans are best known for their black teas; the Japanese specialize in green teas, and the Chinese make all four kinds.

India and Sri Lanka

Darjeeling—known as the "tea of mountain mists"—grows high on the foothills of the Himalayan range, where its bushes are wreathed with the damp, clean air of the mountainside. The height and the coolness are crucial to this champagne of teas. The slow growth produces leaves of a delicate power with hints of Muscat grapes, perfumed roses, and citrus fruits. A fine, white cup of pale gold Darjeeling drunk without milk, is the captivating queen of drinks: beautiful, regal, and flirtatious.

Some Darjeeling teas are labeled with the name of the tea garden they come from, such as Castleton, Tukdah, Margaret's Hope, and Badamtam. These places, through the soil and the specific growing conditions, give interesting variations in taste in the same way that vineyards give character to wine. First-flush teas, sought by tea-lovers as soon as they go on sale in the spring, are the lightest and most refreshingly aromatic.

Assam teas, grown in the northeast of India, come from the native Indian tea plant, with leaves that are slightly less sweet than the Chinese plant. The teas are invigorating, malty, strong, full-bodied, and sometimes almost spicy. The highlands of southern India, such as the Nilgiris, are also famed for their fine, fragrantly fruity teas, some of which are comparable in style to Ceylon teas.

The best teas from Sri Lanka, still marketed under the island's former name of Ceylon, are also high-grown and include those from the highest tea-producing region on the island, Nuwara Eliya. Each of the six regions—Dimbula, Nuwara Eliya, Uva, Kandy, Galle, and Ratnapura—produces tea of a different character, due to their individual climates and growing conditions.s

China

"All the tea in China" encompasses an astonishing range. The longevity of the Chinese tea-drinking habit has resulted in thousands of categories of teas, some still handmade, using the skills and traditions passed down through families for generations.

Chinese green teas can be shaped into distinctive forms, such as little pellets of Gunpowder tea, which rattle into the teapot like shot, or elegantly arched Chun Mee, also known as Precious Eyebrow tea. Some prized teas are grown amid fruit blossom or mountain orchids, and the best jasmine teas are made by putting closed flowers into the tea boxes overnight, when they will open and impart their heady scent to the tea leaves. The flowers are discarded and the process repeated several times.

Chinese black teas are often softly fragrant and refreshing, such as the rolled Keemuns with their red-brown liquor, and teas from the provinces of Yunnan and Szechuan, with hints of almonds, flowers, and spices. Tarry black Lapsang Souchong is a smoked tea made by withering and drying the leaves over pine fires.

Oolong teas are some of the most sophisticated of all China's teas. Look out, also, for the rare white teas, such as Silver Needles.

ABOVE Tea bricks, a traditional method of transporting tea, are today made from compressed tea dust and enjoyed for their decorative value. In the past they were also used as currency in exchange for imports.

Japan

Japanese tea is the white wine of brews—a fine, fragrant, pale drink that shines in your cup with a greenish-gold light. In a country with such a sophisticated visual sense and palate, color and delicacy of taste are important.

The finest Japanese tea, Gyokuro (Precious Dewdrop) transforms production into an art form, with the bushes shaded so the leaves produce extra chlorophyll, resulting in a beautiful jade tea with a fresh, herbaceous taste that is smoothly fragrant, sweet, and deep. The renowned powdered tea, Matcha, is made from Gyokuro and is whisked into an astringent frothy green tea to be drunk in the famous Japanese tea ceremony.

Sencha is the high-quality grade of Japanese green tea and can be labeled with the place of origin. The leaves are carefully harvested and steamed after picking so they retain a deep green color that is accompanied by an appealing freshness of taste. The grassy-tasting early teas of the season are much prized and given as presents.

Bancha is an everyday drink that can be made from leaves harvested when the tea bushes are shaped, and Kukicha uses large leaves and stems. Genmaicha includes puffed rice, which mellows the green tea. Hojicha is a roasted tea, whose smoky, savory strength makes it a good partner for Japanese food.

ABOVE LEFT Genmaicha tea, made with puffed rice to give a mellow, easy-drinking Japanese tea with a toasty, buttery, nutty flavor.
ABOVE RIGHT Matcha is the powdered tea used in the Japanese tea ceremony.

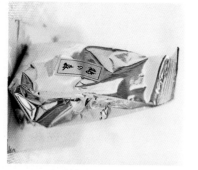

other specialties

Taiwan is famous for its oolong teas, traditionally known as Formosa oolongs from the island's former name. The word "oolong" means "black dragon," after the story of a planter who, following his nose to a delicious fragrance, found a tea bush with the lucky omen of a serpent curled around it. He made tea with the leaves and was captivated by their uniquely sensual scent and savor. Being semi-oxidized teas, oolongs are, in fact, defined by the method of production rather than a particular plant. However, like the leaves in the story, they delight drinkers with their floral notes, hints of fruity fragrance, and peachlike beauty. The teas range from lightly oxidized oolongs, such as Jade Oolong and Pouchong, though to dark oolongs such as White Tip or Oriental Beauty. Some of the most famous Taiwanese oolongs, such as Tung Ting, come from the mountainous area in central Taiwan.

Puerh, a sweet, earthy, aged black tea from the Chinese province of Yunnan, has developed a cult following for its health-giving properties and is sold as loose leaves or molded into shapes.

tea blends

Dedicated tea merchants create and maintain house blends, tasting and mixing teas that vary according to where they come from and even the specific day of harvest, to make sure they have a consistent and distinctive character.

English Breakfast tea might include malty Assams and full-flavored Ceylon and African teas in a blend designed to stand up to a hearty breakfast. Irish Breakfast blends suit the traditional national taste for a strong, dark, punchy brew. Afternoon Tea blends tend to be lighter, perhaps mixing Darjeelings with aromatic black Chinese teas.

An aristocratic classic, Earl Grey tea is flavored with the oil of the citrus bergamot fruit. Russian Caravan teas imitate the taste of the smoky teas that were carried on the long trek from China. Fragrant floral teas such as rose, jasmine, and violet use dried petals to make delicate, delicious cupfuls. Other flavored teas might include such ingredients as dried citrus peel and spices.

It is engaging—and easy—to create your own blends at home with a spoonful of this and a spoonful of that, perhaps using a black tea as a base for color and body, enlivened with a fragrant oolong, a Darjeeling or a smoky souchong, or with the addition of flowers, citrus peel, or dried fruits for a modern flavored blend.

infusions

Like tea, other plants have been infused in water and consumed for centuries for their specific and general medicinal qualities. Chamomile, famous as a relaxing infusion, was used in Roman times to ease period pains. Crushed fennel seeds ease stomach gas in children and adults. Ginger is one of the most ancient remedies for colds. Russian cosmonauts have taken ginseng to protect them from infection when confined together in space, and people use it to increase their energy. Aromatic hops promote sleep. Lavender has been used for tension and halitosis. Nettles, one of nature's diuretics, suck goodness from the soil to be transplanted into your cup. Rosemary has potent aromatic oils for concentration and energy, and acts as an antioxidant. Thyme helps with headaches and works as an antiseptic. Vervain is prized by the food-loving French for liver problems and aids the digestion. Refreshing mint is a digestive drink that soothes you into a sweet night's sleep. And scented lemon verbena, taken for indigestion and nerves, is also drunk simply because it tastes so good.

the tasting

From the gentility of English afternoon tea to the elaborations of the Japanese tea ceremony, there are many ways to enjoy tea. It is easy to get the maximum taste by knowing how to make your brew just right, how different teas can be paired with food, and even how to use these special leaves as a fragrant and interesting ingredient in cooking.

Tea is best kept in an airtight container in a cool, dry place, which is why metal tea caddies, of many decorative designs, are excellent for storing tea leaves.

buying and storing

Specialized tea retailers offer a wide range of well-sourced teas, including their own blends, and will be able to give you advice on what to explore and enjoy. Years of experience can lie behind the counters of such shops: use it, and your efforts will be repaid in every cupful. Tea keeps well, so it is worth going to a full-fledged tea merchant or ordering on the internet every so often to stock up.

Store tea away from sunlight and heat in airtight caddies or simply in the packs fastened at the top of the leaves with a bag clip. To enjoy the freshest taste, ideally use green tea within six months and black tea within a year or so. Tea keeps best of all in larger quantities, which is why specialized suppliers have big containers from which they weigh out the leaves for each purchase.

When you buy Indian and Ceylon teas, "FOP" means Flowery Orange Pekoe (pronounced "peck-oh"), referring to the delicate bud and top leaf at the end of each shoot. This indicates a high grade of tea. "Pekoe" comes from the Chinese word for "white down" and refers to the appearance of the furled new leaf, and Orange began as an honorific reference to the Dutch princes of Orange. Grading can go all the way up to SFTGFOP—Special Finest Tippy Golden Flowery Orange Pekoe—quite literally a tiptop tea. "Orange Pekoe" means the next leaf down and is also a good grade of tea. Broken teas of all grades have a "B" in their label and make stronger, darker brews for a more bracing breakfast drink.

equipment

China is a good material for teapots and cups because it retains the heat of the brew but does not alter its flavor. Glass pots are a modern alternative and let you see the whole leaf tea unfurl as the tea brews. Look for a pot with a handle you can hold easily without burning your fingers and with a lid that will stay on when pouring. The first teapots in the world were made in Yixing in China, at a time when tea-drinking evolved from powdered, whipped tea to infusing whole leaves in water. These beautiful pots of unglazed stoneware are still made today, and over time, the porous material becomes infused with the flavor of the tea.

A plain white china cup shows off the colors that distinguish different teas, such as the green-gold of Japanese teas and the delicate clarity of first-flush Darjeelings. To brew a single mug of loose-leaf tea you can also use an infuser mug with a removable mesh basket or an infuser ball.

Teapots are now available with infuser baskets for the leaves, which you can remove after the tea has been brewed for the right length of time to prevent it from stewing. You can also brew the tea Chinese-style in a tea bowl, refreshing the leaves with new water for successive brews.

making the perfect cup

How you brew your tea is ultimately down to your personal taste, and the specific leaves and brewing vessel you are using, so experiment with the guidelines listed below to see what method works best for you.

• For black and oolong teas, you need about one rounded teaspoon of whole leaves per cup, and slightly less for broken, unless you like strong tea. For green tea and fine white teas, use about two rounded teaspoons per cup.

• Use freshly run cold water and bring it to a boil. Turn off the kettle or remove the pan as soon as the water boils, otherwise it becomes de-oxygenated and the resulting brew will be less bright in flavor.

• Warm the pot—or cup, if using an infuser—by swilling hot water around the inside, then pouring it away.

• Pour the just-boiled water on black and oolong teas, but for green and white teas, leave the water until it is slightly cooler (150–175°F, and even lower, around 120°F for Gyokuro) before pouring onto the leaves. Leave the boiled water in the pan or kettle for two to three minutes to get it to around 175°F.

• Black tea needs about five minutes' brewing for whole leaves, two to three for broken. Fine Darjeelings need about two or three minutes. Green tea needs two to three minutes. Oolongs need about seven minutes, and white about ten. Tea left on the leaves too long, especially green tea, becomes astringent and bitter.

adding citrus fruit, milk, and sugar

Many people add a slice of lemon to black tea. However, some fine, first-flush Darjeelings taste remarkably lemony even without this addition. As a change, try a slice of orange in an aromatic tea such as Earl Grey.

The contentious question of adding tea to milk, or milk to tea, has vexed tea drinkers, especially in Europe, for generations. Some say milk was originally put in first to protect the precious early china teacups from the heat. It mixes better with the tea and stops fats from being scalded and developing a "cooked" taste. Others believe that adding the milk to the tea helps you to judge the right amount to put in. Brisk, strong black tea such as Assam or blends such as English Breakfast are designed for the Western habit of adding a drop of milk. However, milk can muffle the delicate aromas and flavors of a sophisticated tea such as a first-flush Darjeeling. It is unsuitable for the subtle freshness of green and oolong teas, and is as inconceivable with the ultra-fine white teas as it would be with herbal infusions.

The Russians will sometimes take a spoonful of jam in tea, and it is a custom both there and in the Middle East to drink tea through a sugar lump held between the teeth or dissolving in the mouth. Sugar takes the edge off subtle teas, but a spoonful of sugar or honey can bring out the flavor of herbal infusions and teas such as North African mint tea.

tea and food

Teas and foods have evolved to suit each other. Small, thirst-quenching cupfuls of jasmine-scented green tea are constantly poured by the Chinese to partner food, and dim sum developed in the teahouses of Canton as snacks to eat with tea at any time of the day before dinner. The British need strong, black tea to go with fried breakfasts, fish and chips, and the tea-break "biscuit," while the elegance of afternoon tea brings out fine china, crustless sandwiches, and Darjeeling. Japanese green teas, with their refreshing, savory edge, are perfectly suited to drinking with foods such as sushi and sashimi. The Russians took to having an ever-ready samovar so tea could sustain them before and after their main meal of the day.

As an ingredient in food, tea is valued for its flavor and colour. The Chinese lightly crack the shells of hard-cooked eggs and simmer them in tea and soy sauce to marble the whites with dark veins. For a famous Szechuan dish, duck is smoked in a wok over a smoldering mixture of tea, sugar, and rice. The Japanese use the bright green of powdered tea to make green-tea ice cream. The Burmese eat tea pickled, in a dish called *lepet*, to revive them at the end of meals.

Tea also adds fragrance to sweet dishes, from jam and jelly to refreshing sorbets. Home bakers plump up dried fruit in tea to make teabreads; modern fusion chefs coat exotic fruits in spiced tea syrups, and fine French chocolatiers use such flavors as Earl Grey and jasmine tea in their smooth scented ganaches.

tea and health

Tea was first consumed for its beneficial, reviving properties, and science has proved what folk medicine knew all along. In addition to containing minerals and vitamins, tea has a good dose of polyphenols, which act as antioxidants, mopping up the free radicals that damage the body. These polyphenols are particularly potent in green tea, which is why it is promoted as such a healthy drink. Tea is thought to act against such problems as heart disease, cancer, and tooth decay.

Tea has less caffeine per cup than coffee, but if you want to lessen the caffeine content in your tea, infuse for as short a time as possible, drink green tea (apart from Japanese Matcha, which has a buzz), or pour away the first brew and re-use the leaves so there will be less of the water-soluble caffeine in the next brew.

chai masala

This spiced Indian tea can be used to ward off and relieve colds, but has become popular in the West as a delicious drink in its own right.

½ cup milk

2 teaspoons sugar

1 teaspoon black tea

¼ teaspoon freshly ground nutmeg

¼ teaspoon finely grated fresh ginger or a pinch of ground ginger

3 cloves

seeds of 3 green cardamom pods

a pinch of ground cinnamon

makes 2 small cups

Put 1 cup water with the milk and sugar in a saucepan. Add the tea and spices. Bring to a boil, reduce the heat, and simmer for 2 minutes. Strain into cups and serve.

You can play around endlessly with the proportions and ingredients in the spice mixture to suit your own taste. Use dried rather than fresh ginger if you are making a larger quantity, and give the mix a shake before use to redistribute the spices.

This adaptation of the famous Szechuan tea-smoked duck uses the enjoyable technique of home-smoking in a wok. Apply the same principle to smoke foods such as shrimp, fish, and tofu, using teas such as jasmine and Earl Grey.

tea-smoked chicken

Put the peppercorns, salt, star anise, and cinnamon into a dry wok or skillet and toast over medium heat until the pepper smells aromatic and the salt becomes light brown. Discard the star anise and cinnamon. Using a mortar and pestle, grind the salt and pepper to a fine powder. Rub the mixture lightly over the chicken, cover, and chill overnight in the refrigerator to develop the flavors.

Line the wok with a double layer of foil. Put the rice, sugar, and tea into the wok and toss gently. Put the metal rack over the tea mixture.

Remove the chicken from the refrigerator and sprinkle all over with soy sauce. Transfer the breasts to the rack (they should not touch the smoking mixture). Cover the wok tightly with a lid and put over a high heat until you see smoke rising from under the lid. Reduce the heat to low and continue smoking for 15 minutes. Turn the heat off and continue smoking, without lifting the lid, for a further 15 minutes.

Remove 1 breast from the wok and slice to check if it is cooked. If not, continue smoking. To serve, cut each breast into 6–7 slices and serve with rice or noodles and stir-fried vegetables.

1½ teaspoons Szechuan peppercorns

1½ tablespoons sea salt

2 whole star anise

1 cinnamon stick, broken into large pieces

6 skinless, boneless chicken breasts

2 tablespoons soy sauce

Smoking mixture:

½ cup white rice (any kind)

½ cup white sugar

2 tablespoons black tea

Wok with rack and lid
Foil

serves 6

Fragrant teas make delicious sorbets. Try this recipe with different teas, including modern fruit and flower varieties such as passionflower, or traditional blends such as Earl Grey.

jasmine tea sorbet

2 tablespoons jasmine tea

¼ cup plus I level tablespoon sugar

freshly squeezed juice of ½ orange

freshly squeezed juice of I lime

Serves 4

Make the tea as usual, using 1½ cups boiling water and infusing for 3 minutes. Put the sugar into a bowl. Pour the hot tea over the sugar and stir until dissolved. Let cool.

Add the fruit juices to the tea mixture, then churn in an ice-cream maker, according to the manufacturer's instructions.

Serve immediately or freeze. If frozen, soften for a few minutes in the refrigerator before serving. This is an intensely flavoured ice, so serve in modest portions, about 2 tablespoons per person in small glasses.

Japanese tea ceremony

The Japanese tea ceremony, or "way of tea" is a ritual consisting of the making, serving, and drinking of tea. The guests come through a garden of plants and pathways to enter the teahouse after rinsing their hands and mouth, a gesture of purification. They are served food of seasonal ingredients, colors, and shapes, and two kinds of tea by a tea practitioner.

The tea served is Matcha, the finest powdered green tea, which is mixed with hot water in the tea bowl, using a small whisk of split bamboo. The first brew is thick, and each guest, in turn, takes a few sips from the shared vessel. The principal guest will ask the name of the tea; then the character of the utensils and tea bowl is appreciated by the participants. Little colorful Japanese sweetmeats are made to be eaten with the tea and appeal to all the senses with their appearance, texture, smell, taste, and the sound of the poetry of their names. The second, thinner tea is served in individual bowls, whisked to have a frothy top.

Every movement, every utensil, every detail—from the incense on the charcoal fire on which the water boils to the way the tea bowl is held—build into the overall meaning of the event. At its center, the ritual embodies the qualities of respect, harmony, sharing, and consideration that are at the heart of hospitality in every culture.

British afternoon tea

"Nowhere is the English genius of domesticity more notably evidenced than in the festival of afternoon tea," wrote the novelist George Gissing. The British took to tea with an enthusiasm second to none in the Western world.

Forty percent of every drop of liquid drunk in Britain still comes in the form of "a cuppa"—a total of 165 million cups a day. The great comforter, reviver, source of solace, and warmer of the British soul, tea even has its own mealtime in the form of afternoon tea. This institution gained popularity in the 19th century as the evening meal was served later, leaving a hungry gap as the clock struck five.

The meal has developed its own selection of edible delicacies. Sandwiches can be cucumber,

cream cheese and walnut, or watercress, or sweet with preserves or honey. The cakes might include an angelically light cake, a dark fruitcake, a rich chocolate cake, or a sticky gingerbread. Perhaps the tea table might be spread with sugary cookies, crumpets dripping with golden butter, scones with clotted cream and strawberry jam. Ham and eggs and other "real" foods may be served for the more substantial "high tea," which replaces an evening meal altogether.

The teapot crowns the regal tea set, displayed on a white tablecloth in the living room or on a garden table in summertime. But afternoon tea is still taken, even if it is just a cup and a candy bar in front of the computer.

Earl Grey punch

2 tablespoons Earl Grey tea
freshly squeezed juice of 1 lemon
1¼ cups orange juice
½ cup plus 2 tablespoons apple juice
1 cup gingerale
1 tablespoon sugar
2 sprigs of mint
10 ice cubes
dark rum, to taste (optional)

Makes about 1 quart

Put the tea in a teapot. Measure 1¼ cups boiling water and pour it over the tea. Set aside to infuse for 4 minutes.

Meanwhile, pour the fruit juices, gingerale, and sugar into a pitcher. Add the infused tea and stir to dissolve all the sugar. Add the mint.

Let cool, then chill in the refrigerator. Remove the mint and serve in the pitcher with ice cubes added. Alternatively fill 4 glasses with ice cubes and pour over the punch. If you are using rum, stir into the punch before adding the ice.

The tea in this fruit punch recipe stops the drink from being too sweet and makes it all the more refreshing. In turn, the punch adds a wonderful fragrant edge to this fruit salad.

Earl Grey winter fruit salad

8 dried pears
12 dried apricots
1¼ cups Earl Grey punch
1 tablespoon sugar
1 tablespoon ground ginger
4 apples, peeled, cored, and quartered
3 pears, peeled, cored, and quartered
heavy cream, to serve

serves 6

Cut each dried pear lengthwise into 3 pieces. Put the dried pears and apricots and the punch into a bowl, cover, and chill for at least 2 hours, or overnight in the refrigerator. Transfer the plumped-up fruits and punch to a saucepan, then add the sugar, ginger, apples, and pears. Bring to a boil, lower the heat, and simmer for about 5 minutes, until the fruit is tender but firm.

Cool and serve with cream.

tea in North America

The tea-drinking habit was probably brought to the east coast of the United States by Dutch settlers. Tea pleasure gardens sprang up, where people could meet, drink, walk, see, and be seen. After the Boston Tea Party and other such events, patriots shunned tea in favor of other infusions. But, although coffee has become more of a national drink, tea is still popular in the North America, and no less a person than George Washington was an avid imbiber.

The United States gave the world the tea bag, which was created by New York tea merchant Thomas Sullivan, who sent out single samples of tea in little silk bags and was astonished when customers asked for supplies not just of the tea, but of the bags, too.

In recent years, alongside quality coffee, there has been a surge of interest in leaf teas in the North America. Many specialists have opened stores and internet mail-order services, offering the likes of estate first-flush Darjeelings, fragrant oolongs, interesting Chinese leaves, health-giving green teas, and own-label blends, from breakfast teas to chai masala.

iced tea

Iced tea was first presented to the world at the St. Louis World Fair in 1904.

The basic principle is to make strong tea—twice as much tea as you would normally use—and pour it over ice cubes (about 3–4 per glass) into a pitcher. To this you can add any number of ingredients to taste, such as freshly squeezed orange, lemon, or lime juice, and sugar, again to taste. Alternatively, add herbs or spices, such as mint or finely grated fresh ginger. Iced green tea is refreshingly delicious, too, and you can experiment with fragrant floral blends.

Iced tea can also be made by putting tea in water and leaving it out in the sun. For clear, rather than cloudy, iced tea, infuse the leaves in cold water overnight in the refrigerator.

The North African way is to pour this tea from a great height, creating bubbles on the top of the drink. Mint tea is traditionally drunk in small, often decorative, glasses that are frequently replenished, and can be accompanied by delicious, sticky-sweet pastries. Simply multiply the ingredients given below according to the number of people you are serving.

North African mint tea

2 teaspoons Chinese green tea, such as gunpowder

1 sprig of mint (spearmint is authentic, but other mints will do)

¼–1 teaspoon white sugar, to taste

Serves 1

Put the green tea and mint in a teapot. Pour 1 cup just-boiled water into the pot and leave to infuse for 3 minutes. Strain the mint tea into a glass or cup. Stir in sugar to taste. Some people like to put pine nuts into the glass: they soften as they soak and are eaten at the end.

Bodum Café and Home Store
413–415 West 14th Street
New York NY 10014
(212) 367 9125
www.bodum.com

Choice Organic Teas
Granum Inc
2414 SW Andover Street
Seattle WA 98106
(206) 525 0051
www.choiceorganicteas.com

East Teas
31 Bradmore Park Road
London W6 0DT, UK
00 44 20 8741 3671
00 44 20 7394 0226
enquiries@eastteas.com

Grace Tea Company
50 West 17th Street
New York NY 10011
(212) 255 2935
www.gracetea.com

Harney & Sons Fine Teas
PO Box 665
Salisbury CT 06068
(888) 427 6398
www.harney.com

HR Higgins
79 Duke Street
London W1K 5AS, UK
00 44 20 7629 3913
www.hrhiggins.co.uk

Imperial Tea Court
1411 Powell Street
San Fransisco CA 94133
(415) 788 6080

Great Wall Shopping Mall
18230 East Valley Hwy 135
Kent WA 98032
(425) 251 8191
www.imperialtea.com

In Pursuit of Tea
224 Roebling Street
Brooklyn NY 11211
(718) 302 0780
www.truetea.com

Layton Fern & Co Limited
Superlative teas & coffees since 1893
(+44) 1256 355661
www.coffeeisferns.co.uk

Mariage Frères
70 Av des Terroirs de France
75012 Paris, France
(+33) 1 43 47 1854
www.mariagefreres.com

McNulty's Tea and Coffee
109 Christopher Street
New York NY 10014
(212) 242 5551
www.mcnultys.com

Peet's Coffee and Tea
PO Box 12509
Berkeley CA 94712-3509
(510) 594 2100
www.peets.com

The Republic of Tea
(800) 298 4832
www.republicoftea.com

Serendipitea
32-29 Greenpoint Avenue
Long Island City NY 11101

(718) 752 1444
www.serendipitea.com

Simpson & Vail
PO Box 765
3 Quarry Road
Brookfield CT 06804
(800) 282 8327
www.svtea.com

Stash
PO Box 910
Portland OR 97207
(800) 547 1514
www.stashtea.com

Teacup
2207 Queen Anne Avenue
Seattle WA 98109
(206) 283 5931
www.teacup.safeshopper.com

Tealuxe
108 Newbury Street
Boston MA 02116
(617) 927 0400
www.tealuxe.com

Teas of Green
www.teasofgreen.com

Tenren Teas
15 stores in US and 115 worldwide
(650) 583 1044
www.tenren.com

The Tea Man's Tea Talk
www.teatalk.com

Upton Tea Imports
34A Hayden Rowe Street
Hopkinton MA 01748

(800) 234 8327
www.uptontea.com

Urth Caffe
8565 Melrose Ave
West Hollywood CA 90069
(310) 253 7788
www.urthcaffe.com

Whittard's T-Zone
38 Covent Garden Market
London WC2E 8RF, UK
00 44 20 73796599
(866) 479 7723 for customer services
www.whittard.com

FAIR TRADE ORGANIZATIONS

The Fair Trade principle is a commitment to setting new standards for commercial trading in developing countries.

Equal Exchange
251 Revere Street
Canton MA 02021
(781) 830 0303
www.equalexchange.com

Teadirect and Cafédirect
City Cloisters
Suite B2, 196 Old Street
London EC1V 9FR, UK
020 7490 9520
www.cafedirect.co.uk

Transfair
1611 Telegraph Avenue, Suite 900
Oakland CA 94612
(510) 663 5260
www.transfairusa.org

index

acknowledgments

I'd like to thank everyone I have talked to about tea, particularly Tim d'Offay and Alex Fraser, of the excellent East Teas, who sell in London's Borough Market and by mail, and Giles Hilton of Whittards and Maurizio at the Whittards T-Zone in Covent Garden, London (the upstairs room is a calm space in a busy place). At Ryland Peters & Small, I'd like to thank Alison Starling, Sophie Bevan, Luis Peral-Aranda, Gabriella Le Grazie; and Emily Chalmers and Debi Treloar for making the pictures so beautiful and real. Thanks to Julia Brown for loans from her collection. Thank you to all those at HR Higgins, a fine tea and coffee shop in London, for their help with the photographs. Thanks, in general, to my aunt Julia Ellis for bringing me packets and tales from her travels, and to Gail and Frances for book hunting.

PICTURE CREDITS
Page 7: Plucking tea, Herkulu Estate, Tanzania, by Niall McGarry © Cafédirect.

café**direct**

The publisher would like to thank Layton Fern and HR Higgins for allowing us to photograph their shops.

CHINA FUJIAN OOLO